Andrew Fleming

Blood Stains in Criminal Trials

Andrew Fleming

Blood Stains in Criminal Trials

ISBN/EAN: 9783743325562

Manufactured in Europe, USA, Canada, Australia, Japa

Cover: Foto ©ninafisch / pixelio.de

Manufactured and distributed by brebook publishing software
(www.brebook.com)

Andrew Fleming

Blood Stains in Criminal Trials

BLOOD STAINS

IN

CRIMINAL TRIALS.

BY

ANDREW FLEMING, M. D.

PITTSBURG:
1861.

Republished from the American Journal of the Medical Sciences.

PRINTED BY
W. S. HAVEN.

CONTENTS.

APPEARANCE OF BLOOD STAINS.

I. CHEMICAL EXAMINATION OF BLOOD STAINS.

STAINS WHICH MAY BE CONFOUNDED WITH BLOOD STAINS.

II. MICROSCOPICAL EXAMINATION OF BLOOD STAINS.

BLOOD STAINS.

—.•.—.— .—

In the trial of criminal cases, especially where the evidence is of a circumstantial character, it is frequently of the greatest importance to determine of what certain spots are composed, in order to fix the guilt or attest the innocence of the accused. To this end science has been employed, and frequently, by the weight of her testimony alone, has acquitted the innocent or condemned the guilty. Without any desire to magnify her office, it is a high tribute to science to know that she can by her powers aid in fastening the guilt on him who, under covert of darkness and in the stillness of the night, steals upon his victim, while in calm and peaceful slumber, and for sordid lucre or revenge commits the crime of murder. This duty naturally and properly belongs to the medical man, who possesses a knowledge of physiology, chemistry and microscopy, which befits him for the examination of organic substances. The vocation of the expert thus employed, who stands as an acolyte to justice, is one of honour and high responsibility, for by insufficient knowledge or experience he may, by his evidence, form a link in the chain of testimony which consigns the innocent to punishment or sets free the violator of law.

To arrive at conclusions fraught with such salutary and terrible consequences, it is a sacred duty to use every means in our power; to take advantage of every circumstance, however trivial, in order to prove, beyond the question of doubt, of what certain colouring matter is composed, which has stained clothing, weapons, &c., that may be brought into court, corroborative of crime. Before advancing to the plans and formulæ by which these ends are to be attained, it would be well to have in the mind the character of the substance whose correlative it is proposed to examine. The blood is an almost homogeneous fluid, endowed, while under the catalytic influence of the vessels, with a property closely resembling vitality, and bearing the elements out of which the various structures are to be developed or sustained, and from which the glands elaborate their special secretions. The variety of its numerous attributes indicates the complexity of its nature. Owing to its complexity, and the absolute certainty required in medico-legal investigation, arises the difficulty of the examination of suspicious stains.

Appearance of Blood Stains.—The colour of blood stains depends on their age, the material on which they are deposited, the quantity of blood effused, and the circumstances of moisture and temperature to which they have been subjected. If the substance upon which blood is allowed to fall is highly polished—such as metal, porcelain, and varnished wood—the stains, which will be dark-brown shining masses, easily removed, present cracks, radiating from the centre. Shallow stains upon white or porous substances are of a lighter shade when of the same age; yet, when the clots are large, the blood forms for itself a base, upon which the surface presents the same appearance as when on a polished substance. It is impossible to know the age of blood stains by their appearance, as it is so much modified by various contingencies. The colour is altered by being deposited on substances which modify it; and the presence of blood stains, when small, upon clothing, furniture, &c., cannot in some cases be ascertained by examination with sunlight. Dr. Ollivier, d'Angers,[1] was summoned one evening, in March, 1833, to examine without delay certain premises, and furniture therein, where it was thought a murder had been committed upon a woman, whose body had been found upon the street, and there deposited, it was supposed some days after death. Accompanied by Dr. Pillon, he proceeded forthwith to the house, supposing that it would be impossible to discover blood stains by candlelight; but, fortunately, this proved the means of their discovery. The furniture, the paper-hangings, which had a pale-blue ground, and the chimney-piece, which was painted black, had been carefully examined in daylight, without anything peculiar being noticed. On bringing the candle close to the wall-paper, a large number of small spots, of a dirty red colour, the fourth of a line in diameter, were discovered, that by day had the appearance of black points, which were confounded with those making part of the figures on the paper. By the same means spots were found on the furniture, and a large one on the chimney-piece. The next day these observations

[1] Archives Générales, ii. sér., t. i. p. 431.

2

were verified by MM. Lesueur and Barruel, who were obliged to resort to artificial light to find the spots.

I. Chemical Examination of Blood Stains.

The chemical properties by which the presence of blood, whether belonging to man or any other warm-blooded animal, is established, are owing chiefly to the reaction of its peculiar colouring matter. In the examination of suspicious stains it is well to note their absolute and relative position, their form, size, and thickness, and, when upon linen, woollen, or other stuffs, to number or designate them in some way as belonging to some particular part, especially of clothing, for the position of them is frequently corroborative of the manner in which the crime has been committed. It is necessary to put a mark on weapons which have been examined, in order to again identify them.

When the stains are upon cloth, a piece is cut out, containing the stain, or part of it, to be examined, and suspended by a thread in a test-tube; and if the stain is recent, the red colouring matter will soon be imparted to the water, but if it is old, a longer time is required for its solution. If porous substances, such as wood, stones, mortar, and bricks, with blood stains upon them, are put into water, the blood is dissolved and carried into the depths of the material without giving the colour to water. To overcome this difficulty, it is necessary to rasp or reduce them to powder, and add to water. Stains upon hard substances, whose size renders it inconvenient to dissolve by putting them in water, can be scraped off and then dissolved. In all cases, when upon iron or steel, care should be taken, in removing the stains by water, not to allow the instruments to remain long enough for oxidation to commence.

The characteristics by which blood stains are distinguished from those produced by other substances are the following:—

1. They are soluble in distilled water, and impart to it a beautiful red colour, more or less intense, as the proportion of the size of the stain and water vary, of a very feeble alkaline reaction, changing the red litmus to blue.

2. When ammonia is added to the aqueous solution, no *change* takes place in the colour, but an alteration from red approaching to brown is found, in proportion to the degree of concentration of the ammonia.

3. When the solution is heated, coagulation takes place, the bright red colour is destroyed, and grayish flocculi are formed.

4. These flocculi are quickly dissolved by solution of potassa, and the liquid assumes a green tint by reflected, and red by transmitted light. The dichroism produced in this manner, according to M. Gaultier de Claubry,[1] is *a certain indication of the presence of blood.* When the solution is very dilute, to produce this phenomenon an advantage will be found in using caustic potassa.

5. Blood stains are insoluble in alcohol, ether, chloroform, and oils.

6. Dried blood is slowly soluble in strong sulphuric and muriatic acids, forming dark-brown solutions; it is more rapidly acted upon by nitric acid, which dissolves it with effervescence.

[1] Méd. Légale, p. 783.

A little experience in testing shades and tints of colour, whether of a simple or compound kind, soon demonstrates the difficulty in distinguishing them with accuracy. To avoid this, M. Boutigny[1] has proposed an application of the properties which liquids present in their spheroidal state. Having found that when a drop of water is thrown into a capsule heated to 171° Cent. and higher, the liquid forms a sphere, which neither touches nor moistens the capsule—the temperature of the drop of water is always 96° .5 C., upon whatever surface the phenomenon is produced, and the evaporation, when the capsule is heated to 200° C., is fifty times slower than by ebullition at 100° C.—he applied these principles to blood stains, and takes, for example, a stain having a diameter of 0.001 millimetre, or 0.03937 of an English inch. Next a glass graduate of 0.020 millimetre in length, and 0.002 millimetre in diameter inside, is taken, and the stain then cut out and introduced into the graduate, at a distance of 0.005 millimetre from the bottom, and, by the aid of a pipette, 0.10 gramme, or 1.54 English grains, of cool distilled water is poured upon it. When the stain is completely discoloured, a flat silver capsule is heated to redness over an alcohol lamp, the red liquor is removed by a pipette, and thrown upon the capsule by blowing gently at the extremity of the tube. This operation is scarcely finished before the liquid has lost its transparency, and acquired a grayish-green colour. This liquid is then touched with a glass rod, previously dipped in a solution of caustic potassa, and it immediately regains its transparency, and presents a colour, *sui generis*, green by reflection, and red

[1] Annales d'Hygiène pub., 1844, ii. p. 217.

by refraction. If the liquid is now touched with a rod which has been dipped in hydrochloric acid, it loses its transparency, which it regains by the addition of potassa, and thus almost indefinitely, provided from time to time a drop is added to preserve the original volume of the liquid. This very simple and ingenious method, M. Boutigny says, is equally applicable to large quantities of blood.

Analysis.—From the indirect method by which the expert proceeds in this kind of investigation, it is easy to discover that the results are frequently not of so manifest a character as desirable. Chemical analysis is, however, the only means in our power to determine the composition of suspected stains where putrefaction has taken place, or an attempt has been made to wash them out with a reagent of a kind suitable to destroy the integrity of anatomical elements of the blood. In order to more easily and thoroughly comprehend the analysis of blood stains, it is advisable to consider on which of the components of the blood it is founded, and to have in the mind the characteristics by which they are recognized.

Of the great number of constituents of the blood, but five are essentially concerned in the chemical examination. viz. *Hæmatin, Iron, Nitrogen, Fibrin,* and *Albumen.*

Hæmatin.—It is owing chiefly to the presence of this substance in the blood, that the chemical tests for blood stains are available. This pigment, discovered by Lecanu, and as yet not fully known, gives to the blood its vermilion colour, and, circulating in the minute capillaries of the body, tints the surface with carnation hue. It is contained within the corpuscles, and it is not possible to obtain it in precisely the same condition in which it exists in the blood. When perfectly pure, it is a pulverulent, amorphous mass, of a rich dark-brown colour, and, *when prepared by sulphate of soda and alcohol*, acidulated with sulphuric acid, is *insoluble* in ether, alcohol, water, fatty and volatile oils, but slightly soluble in chloroform. Sulphuric and hydrochloric acids do not affect it, and water combined with either of these, does not dissolve it. Alkaline solutions readily dissolve hæmatin in different proportions. When chlorine is passed over hæmatin, moistened with water, white flocculi are formed, the chlorine combines with it, and chloride of hæmatin is produced. The brilliant colour of perfectly pure hæmatin is instantly destroyed by contact with hypochlorous acid.

It is essential to know if the characteristics of this pigment, as exhibited in blood stains, are susceptible of such modification, by the presence of other substances, as to make it impossible to discover them by ordinary methods of procedure. The most important, from the frequent examination required of steel and iron weapons, is to know that rust formed on these can act in this manner.

J. L. Lassaigne,[1] among the earliest contributions to the literature on this subject, gives his opinion, based upon experiments made with blood stains upon instruments of iron and steel, that the results differ according to the circumstances under which they have been placed. When stained instruments are put in a dry atmosphere and an elevated temperature—conditions favorable to evaporation—the stains are in the form of scales, which present no change in the physical properties of blood; but

[1] Archives Générales de Méd , t. viii. 1825, p. 289.

when in a cold and moist atmosphere—the water of the blood combined with that of the air—there will be produced a film of rust, in which it will be impossible to find the physical properties of dried blood.

By experiments made during a period of nearly thirty years, M. Lassaigne[1] has confirmed these results, and says that this difference is owing to the combination of the colouring and albuminous principles of the blood with the peroxide of iron formed by contact with air and moisture.

The discoveries of M. Lassaigne have been fully attested, in a practical manner, by Prof. H. Rose, of Berlin,[2] in the examination of a knife which was supposed to have served to commit a murder. The crime took place during the summer in a wheat field, where the knife was found a long time afterwards. The blade of it was, by the long-continued exposure on the damp ground, so thickly covered with rust that the metallic polish was to be seen in but a few places. A small quantity being removed by scraping, and slightly heated in a test-tube, developed ammonia, which changed moistened red litmus paper to blue, but, when heated strongly, gave out neither a disagreeable odour nor traces of empyreumatic oil. It was a clasp knife, open, likely, in the manner in which it was found, and perhaps the rain had washed away all the traces of blood.

The inside of the handle of the knife was filled with a dark or almost black substance, which immediately after its extraction was soft, but soon became hard and friable. A small quantity heated in a test-tube behaved as dried

[1] Annales d'Hygiène pub., 2me sér. t. v. 1856, p. 206.
[2] Vierteljahresschrift für prak. Phar., III. B. 2 Heft. s. 209.

blood, developed a strong and disagreeable odour, formed an empyreumatic oil, and from the heated residue, by treating it with carbonate of soda, was shown a considerable quantity of Prussian blue.

When a large quantity of this black substance was treated with cold water, it *did not impart a red colour to the solution*. The digestion was continued for a long time, and aided by a gentle heat, but not sufficiently high to coagulate a solution of albumen, without change. After filtration, a very slight trace of albuminous substance was detected. When this black substance, treated with water and caustic potassa, was boiled, the solution assumed a greenish colour, the filtered liquor showed the characteristic dichroism, and acted with reagents exactly as a solution of colouring matter of the blood with caustic potassa. This solution, digested with hydrochloric acid, dissolved a considerable quantity of oxide of iron, which, after supersaturation with ammonia, fell in the form of a precipitate.

The black substance in the handle was, therefore, chiefly composed of dried blood and oxide of iron, the latter formed as rust upon the iron which lined the sides of the knife. On account of the presence of a large quantity of oxide of iron, the dried blood lost one of its chief peculiarities—solubility in cold water. By a series of comparative experiments, Prof. Rose found that the colouring matter of dried blood is completely precipitated from its solution by hydrated oxide of iron.

A proof of the accuracy of these observations was given by a closer inspection of the knife, when a little piece of wood was seen in the inside, which was probably placed to prevent the point of the blade from striking on the handle. This piece of wood, particularly at the end of it, was covered with stains of blood which probably had not come in contact with the rust. It was transferred to a test-tube containing water, and, after a short time, from the wood, red streaks could be observed falling to the bottom, whilst a flocculent, voluminous matter, of a reddish tint, remained upon the wood, which became whiter the longer the action of the water was continued. The red matter thus obtained proved, by experiment, to be identical with that of blood.

After a long series of experiments, Prof. Rose came to the following conclusions:—

1. When freshly prepared hydrated oxide of iron is digested for twenty-four hours, and at the same time frequently shaken, at a low temperature, with a solution of a blood stain, the filtered solution contains no colouring matter of blood; whilst, by boiling the residue of the filtration with solution of caustic potassa, it is easily detected by the proper reagents.

2. If, in place of hydrated oxide of iron, calcined oxide of iron is treated with a like solution of colouring matter of blood, a considerable quantity will be extracted.

3. Hydrated alumina acts upon blood in precisely the same manner as hydrated oxide of iron, but requires a larger proportion for the same quantity of blood.

4. The detection of colouring matter of the blood is more difficult when it has been allowed to fall upon ground composed of rich garden mould. A weak solution of the colouring matter of the blood with earth of this kind was allowed to digest for several months, when it was found the filtered liquid was colourless, which,

3

evaporated on platina foil, left a slight residue containing no trace of blood. This soil, boiled afterwards with solution of potassa, gave a dark-coloured solution, which was dark-brown after filtration, but, on account of the large quantity of earth taken up by the alkali, it did not show the dichroism which is peculiar to a solution of blood stains with potassa. The solution of earth with potassa, when saturated with acids, forms brown precipitates resembling those formed without blood. In order to recognize the presence of blood in such an alkaline solution of earth, it is saturated with an excess of concentrated chlorine water, when white flocculi appear as in an alkaline solution of blood, whilst in a solution of earth and potassa no such flocculi are seen. If the blood is concentrated, which falls on the ground, these difficulties are not found.

The extended researches of Rose have lately been verified by Dr. G. C. Wittstein,[1] of Munich, who was required to examine several articles of clothing and an axe with its handle, found in the dwelling of a man supposed to be the murderer of a woman, whose body was found in a forest with several wounds on the head and a severe fracture of the skull. The axe and handle appeared to have been washed with some care, and but few stains were noticeable, which, treated, did not furnish satisfactory results. The handle was carefully removed, when it was found as conjectured, that blood had flowed between the wood and iron. The blood, mixed with rust, in this situation, was found to be insoluble in water, proving the assertions of Lassaigne and Rose to be correct.

[1] Vierteljahr. für prak. Pharm., V. B. 3 Heft. s. 382.

To avoid error in the examination of blood stains when mixed with rust or hydrated oxide of iron, I propose the following formula, and by this means, at the same time, add an additional test for blood, based upon the property, which Verdeil[1] has shown hæmatin possesses, of forming, in its alcoholic solution, a lake which is insoluble in a mixture of alcohol and water. Scrape off the mixture of rust and blood, add thereto the smallest quantity of soda, and, with water, make into a thick paste, which transfer to a test-tube containing alcohol; boil for a few minutes, and filter. The filtered liquor contains the colouring matter in solution, which, upon the addition of quicklime in fine powder, falls in the form of a *green* precipitate. For convenience, the solution may be divided in two portions, one of which can be submitted to the ordinary tests for blood. The specific chemical character of the colouring matter of the blood, compared with that of pure hæmatin, varies slightly, owing to the presence of the salts contained in the former.

In the year 1829, M. Morin, of Rouen, was called before a tribunal to decide, whether certain red stains, found upon clothing were produced by human blood, or owing, as pretended by the accused, to fish blood, when he asserted that stains produced by the blood of fishes cannot be confounded with those made by the blood of mammifera. He founded this extraordinary assertion on making some experiment upon the blood of the salmon, by which he found, that acting upon it with sulphuric acid, and supersaturating the latter with magnesia, then treating the coagulum thus formed with boiling alcohol, the colouring

[1] Traité de Chemie Anat., t. iii. p. 383.

matter was dissolved, whilst that of the blood of the mammifera is completely *insoluble* in that vehicle.

It has been shown that M. Morin fell into a grave error in his research, by M. Leeanu,[1] who not only exposed the mistake, but used the same formula to isolate the hæmatin of human blood.

Iron is found in many parts of the body; in several secretions, normal and morbid, and in the blood, where it is intimately associated with hæmatin within the walls of the corpuscles.

Upon superficial examination it would appear that the iron in the blood is in such small proportion that it could not embarrass the chemical analysis of blood stains.

M. Persoz, Prof. of Chemistry at Strasburg, communicated to M. Orfila, that, in the year 1836, to recognize blood stains, he had recourse to hypochlorous acid, which, he said, immediately destroyed all other stains except those formed by rust or blood, which become dark-brown by contact with this acid. After receiving this information, the latter, with M. Cottereau, applied this knowledge practically, and recommended this reagent to MM. Magouty and Loust, of Bordeaux, who were charged with the examination of stains found on the lining of a vest. During the investigation, these gentlemen found that direct stains, or those made by a jet, or by dipping cloths in blood, were different in their action from those produced by contact with a stained body.

From a great number of experiments made on the action of hypochlorous acid, prepared after the formula of Balard—by shaking pure chlorine gas with binoxide of

[1] Annales d'Hygiène pub., t. ix. 1833, p. 226.

mercury, moistened with water—upon various substances, M. Orfila[1] concluded:—

1. That stains made by a mixture of fat and alkanet, fat and charcoal, and madder and oil of poppies, behaved almost in the same manner as blood stains.

2. Hypochlorous acid is completely inefficacious to distinguish blood stains from those made by rust, colcothar, and fat, because the latter remain after a prolonged action of the acid; but they disappear, as Persoz has shown, by the use of a solution of chloride of tin, while blood stains are unaffected by it.

3. That hypochlorous acid is altogether incapable of establishing positively, that a stain is formed of blood, though it can be employed as an accessory means, provided it remains in contact with parts stained, but one or two minutes.

Brame, who performed these experiments, thought that the hypochlorous acid should be perfectly free from perchloride of mercury, as it is easily obtained by Williamson's method, by agitating fresh chlorine with peroxide of mercury. The same author advises removing the stains with faintly alkaline solutions, and then performing the experiments in a test-tube. Buchner states that the presence of mercury does not interfere in the least with the reaction of the acid, and that chloride of lime, chloride of soda, and an addition of muriatic acid, may also be employed.[2]

I have tried the above experiments with hypochlorous

[1] Annales d'Hygie   xxiv. 1845, p. 112.
[2] Liebig's Annalo. American Journ. of Pharm., N. S. vol. xiii. p. 319.

acid made after the method of Balard, Williamson, and Pelouze (the last, by passing dry chlorine over precipitated *red oxide of mercury*, when chloride of mercury and hypochlorous acid are formed; the latter of great purity and concentration), and found the results agreed perfectly with those of Orfila, &c.

Above, I have shown that hæmatin when exposed to the action of hypochlorous acid, is completely decolourized; then to what constituent of the blood is the reaction of this acid owing, and how can the resemblance of its action on blood, colcothar, and rust, be accounted for? To the presence of iron. This is easily proved by the following simple experiment of Dr. F. F. Runge,[1] who has shown that iron can be detected in the most minute particle of blood.

A single drop of blood is received on a linen rag, which is then plunged into a solution of chlorinated lime, which contains hypochlorous acid in small quantity; the red colour is soon changed to yellow and afterwards to a dark brown. The cloth is now carefully washed with pure water, to remove all traces of lime, and the spot treated with an acid (acetic) solution of ferrocyanuret of potassium, when it will be rapidly changed to blue—ferrocyanuret of iron.

To detect the presence of blood by the iron contained therein, when the fabric has been washed, Verghauss[2] has devised the following plan, which, he says, is capable of doing so, indubitably, even with the smallest trace of

[1] Grundrisz der Chem., Th. II. s. 221.
[2] Cannstatt's Jahresbericht für 1845, 1er B. s. 116.

blood. The portion of stained cloth to be examined, is calcined in a platina capsule, the cinder treated with pure sulphuric acid, and the extract tested for iron.

Nitrogen.—This substance, with which we are surrounded on all sides, exists in the body of animals in a gaseous and solid state. Combined with two equivalents of carbon, it forms one of those quasi-simple radicals, cyanogen (C_2N), which has the property of producing salts. The azotized matter of the blood, when submitted to a high temperature, is capable of yielding this in a state suitable to form bases.

C. Wiehr[1] has taken advantage of this and adopted a method to prove blood stains on coloured stuffs, where the solution, tinged by their colour, does not permit the use of reagents; which consists in the generation of cyanide of potassium from the blood stains on the fabrics. After having convinced himself of the absence of wool in the cloth, he calcines a red-coloured, stained piece of the stuff in a porcelain crucible, pulverizes the residue, mixes the powder with carbonate of potassa, and heats the mixture to redness. The mixture is then extracted with water, and to the filtered solution, a small quantity of solution of the salts of protoxide and of sesquioxide of iron, is added: a precipitate of undefined colour is produced, containing the constructed ferrocyanuret (Eisencyanür-Cyanid) of iron and protoxide and sesquioxide of iron, precipitated by the excess of carbonate of potassa used in the process. Dilute sulphuric acid is now added, which dissolves the protoxide and sesquioxide of iron, and leaves behind the ferrocyanuret of iron, undissolved, showing

[1] Handbuch der gericht. Med. von J. L. Caspar. 1857.

now its blue colour. The operation is said to be successful, if a piece of the stained stuff is boiled in caustic lye; the liquid evaporated to dryness and the residue treated in the same way with the salts of iron and sulphuric acid.

Dr. Wolff[1] employed the process, with a successful result, in the examination of blood stains which had remained on linen for a period of twelve weeks.

Fibrin.—This protein body is found in animals in two conditions, solid as found in muscle, and liquid, and perhaps more natural state, in blood and various fluids. When blood is allowed to stand, spontaneous coagulation takes place, and soon after, owing to its presence, a mechanical analysis is found separating the serum from the solid portion.

M. P. Denis[2] was the first person to point out some singular properties possessed by fibrin and its similarity to albumen and casein. By maceration in water containing a neutral salt, for instance, nitrate of potassa, for twenty-four or forty-eight hours, or even longer, according to the proportion of the salt, it will be dissolved. The new product resembles serum and albumen; it precipitates bichloride of mercury, and is coagulated by heat and alcohol. If this saline solution is diluted with water in large quantity, the fibrin will reappear with all its original properties.

The characteristics of fibrin differ, in some degree, from the different sources whence it is derived, and it is held that a difference exists between that of venous and arterial blood. When the former is triturated in a mortar

[1] Cannstatt's Jahr. ber. für 1853, 1er B. s. 15.

[2] Archives Gén. de Méd., t. i. 3me ser., 1838, p. 171.

with $1\frac{1}{2}$ times its weight of nitrate of potassa and the mixture is left for twenty four hours at a temperature of 100°—120°, it becomes gelatinous, slimy, and eventually liquid; in this condition it exhibits all the properties of a solution of albumen, which has been neutralized by acetic acid. With arterial fibrin no such liquefaction happens, and even the fibrin of venous blood, when long exposed to the air or oxygen gas loses the distinction.[1] This discriminative quality belonging to fibrin as obtained from fresh blood, could scarcely be made to serve any purpose in a question as to the origin of blood stains.

When a piece of any material stained with blood to a notable degree, is suspended in water, the colouring matter is quickly dissolved, leaving the fibrin in the form of a grayish mass, with a slight reddish tinge, but which becomes white after continued maceration. This can be removed and submitted to microscopical inspection to determine its identity.

There is one circumstance where it is of the highest importance to be able to discover traces of blood, in which M. Morin[2] thinks he has succeeded. The assassin, in his haste to destroy that which is frequently an essential portion of the evidence against him, washes his clothes with boiling water, sometimes even with the addition of soap, with a view of hastening the disappearance of this indubitable evidence of his crime; whence results the fixation of certain matters of the blood on the tissue. M. Morin experimented with tissues stained with blood, by boiling in water with soap, when it was found the stains were

[1] Liebig, Handwörterbuch der Chem. 1. B. s. 881.

[2] From Journ. de Chim. Méd. Annual of Sci. Dis., 1855.

4

duller than before. Their consistence was always greater than that of the tissue itself; the washings had not perceptibly dissolved the elements of the blood. After reaction for some time with solution of caustic potassa, a liquor is obtained, which is precipitated white by nitric or pure hydrochloric acid, which indicates the solution of one or more of the (protein) matters of the blood. By this alkaline treatment the stain loses some of its colour; but what, then, is the matter which is found in some measure indelibly fixed on the tissue? To solve this question, it is only necessary to put the stained tissue in contact with pure hydrochloric acid, which dissolves the matter of the stain, and forms a solution which, carefully reduced to dryness, furnishes a residue having the property of acquiring a very clear blue colour, with ferrocyanide of potassium, and a blood-red colour, with sulphocyanide of potassium, indicating the presence of iron.

Fibrin has the property of attaching itself to the texture of clothes. Sulphuric acid has the property of dissolving textures made of hemp or linen without altering the fibrin. If, then, a texture of this sort is suspected of being stained with blood, it is to be plunged into concentrated sulphuric acid, which dissolves the texture and leaves the fibrinous part of the blood, presenting a network, where may be distinguished the impressions made by the texture on which the blood was fixed.[1]

Albumen.—In an examination based upon the chemical constituents of the blood, it is necessary to inspect the character of this substance, which is presented in large proportion in the blood, and, like fibrin, variable in quan-

[1] Lancet, 1848, vol. ii. p. 18.

tity in different morbid conditions. The presence of albumen in any fluid can only be proved by its coagulability with heat and nitric acid, because the coagulation by heat can be prevented by numerous substances, both acids and alkalies.

When blood stains have been submitted to the action of water, the albumen is dissolved, and, with the colouring matter, remains in solution. When the solution is heated to 145°, coagulation is seen to take place, and, at the same time, decoloration of the red pigment, one of the chief distinctions of blood. From a number of experiments which I have made upon the decoloration by heat, there appears to be some analogy between it and the coagulation of albumen. If chloride of zinc, corrosive sublimate, tannic and arsenious acids are added to a solution of blood stains, it is changed to a bright-red colour, and, when heat is applied, the decoloration takes place as usual; but when those substances which are known to prevent the coagulation of albumen—such as potassa, soda, lime, baryta, and tartaric, acetic, gallic, citric, oxalic, benzoic, and meta-phosphoric acids—are added, there is no decoloration produced by heat, and, after boiling with these reagents, liquors are obtained of various colours and tints. Thus far the analogy is complete; but when sulphuric acid is added to it, coagulation takes place, but no decoloration is found from the application of heat. The fact that decoloration of a solution of blood by heat may be prevented by the action of various articles, should be remembered by the experimentalist, for frequently attempts are made, with different substances, to destroy the evidences of guilt, which might render invalid the test (3) described above, and produce confusion in the result of the analysis.

II. Zollikofer[1] was a short time ago required to examine whether certain reddish-brown stains, which were found upon a knife, a pair of scissors, on linen, wood, and on the ground, were owing, in a greater or less degree, to the presence of blood. The character of the stains required the employment of a very delicate test in order to obtain reliable results, which was not possible but by adopting as the point of departure the method of II. Rose. His attention was directed chiefly to two of the principal constituents of the blood, viz., albumen and hæmatin. By means of his experiments he found a new and specific reaction of hæmatin, and he is of opinion that by this means he is enabled to generalize the process of II. Rose, which, according to him, is the only one which can be advantageously employed.

When it is required to examine stains upon rusted iron, two varieties are presented for consideration, according to the circumstances under which they have been placed, viz., that where the blood has remained *less* than a month in contact with the rust, and the other where the two substances have been mixed for *more* than a month.

A. *Less than a Month of Contact.*—The rust is carefully scraped into a small porcelain capsule, and allowed to digest for some minutes in cold or slightly warm water. The filtered liquor will then contain the soluble salts of the blood, albumen and hæmatin.

1. The solution is now heated to ebullition. According to the proportion of hæmatin and albumen, a dirty-reddish

coagulum or a simple opalescent cloud is formed. The liquor being slightly alkaline, it is necessary to neutralize it with dilute acetic acid.

2. When the coagulum is dissolved in caustic potassa, the hæmatin liquefies in such a manner as to render the solution dichromatic, green by transmission, and red by reflection.

3. By adding chlorine water in excess either to the dichromatic liquor or to the simple solution (No. 1), there are formed white flocculi (albumen and chloride of hæmatin), which soon separate to the surface of the liquid.

The reaction of No. 2 is indicative of hæmatin alone; the others indicate, at the same time, hæmatin and albumen. When the quantity of blood is very small, the dichromatic appearance is not manifested, even when the chlorine water still produces a perceptible precipitate. In such cases, and to dispel doubts regarding the reagents of H. Rose, he advises to recur to the following consideration, viz.: hæmatin is the only substance which contains iron, and, according to Mulder, $C_{44}H_{22}Az_3O_3Fe$. When hæmatin is dissolved—or, rather, simply suspended—in water, if it be acted on by a current of chlorine, it is precipitated in the form of white flocculi, and loses its iron, which remains in solution in a state of chloride. It is only necessary, in order to detect the latter, to use sulphocyanuret of potassium, which, as is known, is its most reliable and delicate reagent. In operating in this way upon a blood stain which was only two lines in diameter, this chemist has obtained a manifest reaction by the use of sulphocyanuret of potassium, although chlorine water gave simply a whitish cloud, hardly appreciable, which required several hours to precipitate as distinct flocculi.

B. *More than a Month of Contact.*—When blood remains a long time in contact with rust, there is formed, as Rose has shown, a veritable combination, by which hæmatin is rendered insoluble in water. In boiling this compound, it is necessary to avoid a large excess of the alkali, because the saturation will become more difficult.

When this method is employed, it is required to discover, in the first place, if no soluble salt of iron is contained in the spot to be examined. This is easily done by means of sulphocyanuret of potassium, which is agitated with a simple aqueous solution of the stain before it is submitted to the alterative action of potassa. If this reagent detects the presence of iron, two experiments are needed: one which consists in treating the aqueous solution by chlorine, to detect the presence of hæmatin and albumen; the other, by treating the spot first with pure caustic potassa, and supersaturating the solution with chlorine. The iron, separated from the hæmatin by this means, will be found in the product of filtration.

To show that a stain contains iron, cyanogen (materials from which it can be procured), fibrin, or albumen, gives no positive proof of the presence of blood, since these substances are found in many animal and vegetable structures, in various forms and combinations; but to be able to detect them is a valuable auxiliary means to confirm chemical analysis. Of the various tests and methods for the detection of blood, those which are based upon the characteristics which hæmatin possesses are alone of specific value, and in medico-legal investigation should first occupy the attention of the expert. The reaction of hæmatin is the same, whether obtained from arterial or venous blood, and chemistry affords no means of discrimination between these two forms of the vital fluid.

Menstrual blood, in its normal condition, would appear to contain no fibrin, as has been proved by Dr. Letheby,[1] who had an opportunity of examining forty ounces of it in a case of imperforate hymen, and Jul. Vogel, who procured it in a state of purity in a case of procidentia uteri.[2] The instances are frequent in which menstrual fluid possesses all the physical properties of blood, and hence they might be confounded. Nevertheless, where a charge of rape or infanticide has been preferred, and blood stains produced as evidence of the deed, which, on examination, were found to contain no fibrin, the absence of this important constituent of ordinary blood would have some weight in favor of the accused.

To distinguish Human from Animal Blood. — Several methods have been proposed to distinguish, by chemical means, human from animal blood, and the blood of one class of animals from that of another. The most remarkable of these is the plan elaborated by M. Taddei, of Florence, under the name of *hæmatalloscopy*,[3] which is as follows:—

The spots upon weapons, soil, or on furniture, are detached by scraping, the product is weighed in a delicate scale, after which the smallest possible quantity of distilled water is added, and to this a solution of crystallized

[1] Todd and Bowman, Physiol. Anat. and Physiology of Man, Am. ed. p. 848.

[2] Lehmann's Phys. Chemistry, vol. i. p. 631.

[3] Manuel de Méd. Lég., p. 795.

bicarbonate of soda, containing the same quantity, by weight, of the salt as is represented by the weight of the blood. If the liquid has been deposited upon a fabric, it should be separated by water; and, to determine the quantity of it, it is dried at 60° Cent., the cloth to be cut in strips, after which they are macerated in water, or, better, triturated in a mortar with water, and on drying them, and weighing again, the exact quantity of blood will be found, to which the soda, as before, must be added.

A fabric of linen or cotton, which contained hardly 28 to 30 centigram (5 to 6 grains) of dried blood, furnished a quantity sufficient to determine its nature.

After having well shaken the blood with the solution of the bicarbonate, a solution of the sulphate of copper, in very slight excess, is poured into it, and, after ten or twelve hours of repose, the mixture is filtered and washed with care. The filtered liquor is bluish, and the product found in the filter, which is of an olive-green colour, contains the organic substances and the carbonate of copper. The filter is now placed upon bibulous paper, and dried in the sun or in a stove, between two porcelain plates or capsules; the product is detached and triturated in a porcelain mortar before desiccation is completed. M. Taddeï designates this product *powder of interposition*. As this powder is exceedingly hygrometric, it is necessary to protect it from the moisture of the air.

When it is required to determine if a certain quantity of blood belong to man or a vertebrate animal, it is effected by comparison. Ten grains of powder of interposition are accurately weighed, to which are added, in the same capsule, fifteen grains of dilute sulphuric acid, formed with equal parts of acid at 66°, and of water, a mixture to which the author gives the name of *acid liquor.* The capsule is covered with a glass plate, leaving only room at the side for the movement of a glass rod for mixing well the acid and the powder. In operating at 25° or 30° Cent., the powder of interposition, hardly moistened with the acid, changes to olive-green or garnet-red, and from being granular, as it was at first, it now becomes homogeneous, tenacious, pulpy, plastic, and very elastic.

This product, deposited upon a large horizontal sheet of glass, remains in the same state for ten or twelve hours, after which it spreads, adheres to the surface of the glass, becomes shining, and assumes the bright appearance of a melted mass. This appearance is shown upon the lower side of the mass, after four or five hours in summer, and longer in winter. The whole falls lower and lower, the area extends, becomes ordinarily circular, and the substance softens, taking the consistence of an extract. If the continuity is destroyed by means of a glass rod, the rent will soon be filled and the elevations disappear; by gently applying a metallic seal, or a piece of money anointed with oil, the impression is only momentary, and the mass soon regains its first form; on touching it with the finger, it adheres thereto like honey; bibulous paper applied with care to the surface, cannot be elevated without raising some of it, and insects which fall upon the substance remain attached as long as the fresh paste not only can be touched with the finger or blotting paper, but till it can be compressed without adhering. The fluidification increases progressively, the product becomes semi-

5

fluid, and, on inclining the pane of glass to from 20° to 40°, it flows from 80 to 100 millimetres in three or four hours. All the above phenomena are manifested in the space of a day and a half, at a temperature from 25° to 30° Cent., and the fluidification becomes such that, in the space of thirty or forty hours, by inclining the glass to 45°, the mass travels 135 to 160 millimetres in a short time; in fine, after three or four days, the fluidification is complete. In using a rectangular sheet of glass, with a graduated scale upon one of its sides, it is easy to determine the degree of fluidity during a certain period of time at a given inclination.

If the pane of glass upon which the product has been placed is left horizontal until the mass be completely liquefied, it retains its opacity, but becomes so brilliant, and reflects all objects so well, that one can see, as in a mirror, all the points of any body which is presented. If, then, the sheet of glass is turned vertically, and under it a horizontal one, the mass falls on the latter, leaving hardly any trace on the former, so that the objects are delineated behind the vertical sheet in the whole course of the product, which can be made to flow again in the same manner. When the paste is laid on a pane of glass exactly horizontal, after a few days another phenomenon is observed. In the area occupied by the fluid mass, two substances are shown: one solid, granular, whitish, and opaque, the other liquid, diaphanous, of an amber tint, which separates to the periphery, enveloping on all sides the opaque substance, and forming a zone of eight to ten millimetres, with fringed edges. The better to note this effect, the glass should be placed before a window. These substances are easily separated in the following manner: the tare is taken of a trapezoidal, or, better, a hexagonal plate of glass, to which is attached, with a little sealing wax, a very fine brass wire; to this is fixed a piece of filtering paper, cut in a hexagon, a little smaller than the plate of glass, which has been weighed; by means of a pipette, some of the acid liquor is allowed to fall upon it —in quantity, a little more than what is necessary to cover the paper, but still not sufficient to flow beyond— and thereon is sprinkled the powder of interposition. Having taken the whole from the scale, the powder is mixed with the acid by means of a glass rod, and, after several days, the plate of glass is inclined so that the liquid portion flows upon another plate of glass, and is spread on a printed sheet, on which the letters can be easily read through the liquid. The latter is so transparent, that in passing the sun's rays through it, and receiving the image in a camera obscura, there will be found a circle of a beautiful colour, red as fire, bordered by a colourless circle, which is itself surrounded by another obscure one.

On letting some drops of the amber-coloured liquid fall into alcohol at 78° to 82° Cent., the latter is troubled, and a deposit takes place of numerous filaments, of an albuminous appearance, ashy-white or slightly gray, and the liquid becomes a fawn colour; whence it can be concluded that the amber liquor is a combination of acid and hæmatin, with an albuminous or protein substance. One is soluble, the other insoluble, in alcohol.

If some of the liquid is spread upon a plate of glass with the pulp of the finger, it adheres like a fatty or oily substance. If, now, this plate is put into a tumbler filled with distilled water, so that one of its sides touches the bottom and the other the edge, at an inclination of forty-five to fifty degrees, lines traced by the finger will be seen, and, the vessel being in repose, this substance is observed to unite by degrees with the fluid, and form a mass composed of layers which fall to the bottom. If, now, the plate is withdrawn from the liquid, it is seen uniformly covered with a layer of a pearl-white substance, which, rubbed by the finger, unite in small opaque filaments of a deep gray colour. The same result is obtained when the extremity of a glass tube, filled with the fluidified matter, is plunged into water and held vertically in the centre. In placing the latter between the eye and the light, from the end of the tube is seen flowing a very fine filament, which, on breaking, forms small wreaths, attached one to another, that, falling slower and slower, and increasing so much in diameter, they lose their colour, and acquire a refrangibility, almost equal to that of water, which does not longer allow them to be seen. Then the filament which at first, coloured and transparent, occupied the centre of the tube, is opaque, and to the wreath have succeeded white flocculi, which rise and fall in the liquid. This white thread, which remains for some minutes intact and mobile, like the filaments, is formed of albuminous substances of the serum.

If the paste resulting from a mixture of powder of interposition and acid liquor, in the proportion of 1 to 1.5, is allowed to fluidify in the bottom of a conical vessel, and steam directed over it, or a little hot water poured upon it before it is completely liquefied, and allowing the same

to digest with occasional agitation for some time, the solution operates without any clots or threads remaining.
If sufficient carbonate of lime, in fine powder, to saturate
all the acid, is poured into this, and the solution afterwards filtered, the liquid presents a very beautiful lilac or
blue colour, arising from the oxide of copper. By wash-
ing the residue upon the filter until the liquid be scarcely
coloured, and throwing some ammonia upon it, a fluid
passes through of a deep colour—red by refraction, and
greenish-brown by reflection. If the phenomenon is observed in a glass vessel, as the ammonia evaporates, there
is deposited a slight layer of opaque matter on the sides
of the glass, which, when dried, is of an ashy-gray hue,
and dissolves without effervescence in water acidulated
with hydrochloric acid. When completely dried, it is in
the form of a crust, very friable, and of a bottle-green
colour, and which, detached, looks black, and has a metallic lustre. The powder thus obtained is insoluble in
alcohol, but is soluble in that liquid and water when
thereto is added an acid, or, better still, some caustic
alkali. Reduced to paste with one and a half times its
weight of acid liquor, it imparts a garnet-red colour, but
does not form a coherent mass like that formed with the
powder of interposition.

Heat exerts so great an influence upon the fluidification, that the paste made with the powder of interposition
and the acid liquor, in the proportion of 4 to 5, and, consequently, hard and dry, becomes not only of a soft, shining, and semi-fluid appearance, but is completely liquefied
after a few days, when kept at a temperature from 35° to
40° Cent. On the contrary, if the paste is made in pro-

portion of 1 to 1.5, when at 15° Cent., the mass remains without change, or takes the consistence of an extract.

Characteristics of the Blood of Animals.

Ox Blood.—In operating as above described, the plasticity and coherence are found to be less. The mass which is reduced to clots—elastic, but hard and dry, when placed upon a plate of glass, shows no change whatever after thirty hours, either in summer or winter; preserves its form and diameter; neither assumes the consistence of an extract, nor reflects images; and after some weeks, loses its shape when the plate of glass is inclined, takes a darker colour, and alters in firmness so much that the clots become agglutinated, and form masses without consistence, and always granular, whence flows a portion of acid liquor.

Pigeon Blood.—The powder of interposition does not mix with the acid liquor so as to form a homogeneous, plastic, and coherent paste; only a mass of hard and tenacious clots is obtained, which, divided and without cohesion, after some days—aided by a temperature of 25° or 30° Cent.—reunite into a sticky, extractiform, and homogeneous mass.

Green Lizard Blood.—This is with much more difficulty detached from tissues, than the blood of any other animal; whence the cause of the almost indelibility of the spots by water. The powder of interposition does not furnish a coherent and homogeneous mass, but only a pile of clots which do not adhere; at first slightly elastic, they become by degrees moist, flabby, and of a deep colour, afterwards take the brightness and appearance of a semi-fluid substance, and when the agglutination increases rapidly—the temperature being from 30° to 35° Cent.— the clots are united into one brilliant mass, black as pitch, and of an extractiform consistence.

Tench Blood.—The mass made by the powder of interposition and acid liquor, is formed of small clots without cohesion, which do not furnish a plastic and homogeneous substance.

In comparing human blood with that of animals of different classes, it is observed that with the first the powder of interposition yields a consistent, elastic paste of a garnet colour, that softens rapidly and falls like dough in process of fermentation, and having become brilliant, extractiform, dark, and pitchy, it liquefies like syrup, forming large spots with fringed edges, when maintained at a temperature from 30° to 35° C., in a horizontal position; that this paste divides spontaneously into two parts, one liquid, diaphanous, of an amber colour, flowing like water; and the other solid, white, and opaque.

Blood is not human when there is formed an elastic, consistent, and tenacious paste, reducible by pressure to fragments which do not agglutinate, neither fluidify by any means, nor furnish two distinct substances, such, for instance, as ox blood, as the type of the mammifera. In like manner with various other bloods distinct differences are found. In fine, it is human blood alone, which, not forming a homogeneous and coherent mass, whatsoever the proportion of acid liquor may be, gives only isolated clots, not susceptible of forming an emplastic body until several days have elapsed.

To appreciate the degree of fluxility (*fluidifiabilité*) M.

Taddeï uses a tube 0.50 millimetre in length, and from 0.006 to 0.008 millimetre in diameter, closed at one extremity and expanded at the other, like a smoke pipe, and curved at an obtuse angle. When the mass introduced remains several hours, it becomes soft enough to adhere to the glass; the tube is then inclined at an angle of 45°, the mass then flows insensibly, and, by a graduated scale divided into 200 parts, the distance travelled, after three or four hours, is measured. The different kinds of blood by this means are divided in the following manner:—

Coagulable Blood.
- Non fluxible . . . Ruminantia (Ox, deer, &c.).
- Tolerably fluxible
  - Rodentia (Guinea-pig, rabbit, &c.).
  - Solipedes (Ass, horse).
  - Pachydermata (Hog).
  - Quadrumana (Monkey.)
  - Carnivora (Porcupine, pole-cat).
- Very fluxible . . .
  - Carnivora (Cat, fox, dog).
  - Bimana (Man).
  - Rodentia (Rat).

The blood of the dog, man, and the rat, are found placed in the same category, and to distinguish them it is indispensable to compare exactly their degree of fluxility.

To attain the same end, a process has been shown by M. Casanti, who uses as a reagent for the distinction of blood belonging to various animals, phosphoric acid at a density of 1.8, in the following manner: The first step was to establish a distinction between an animal belonging to the mammalia and another vertebrate animal, say a bird. For this purpose, both kinds of blood were carefully dried and treated by an excess of phosphoric acid; the mammalian blood became agglutinated, and formed into a brilliant, homogeneous, and coherent mass; whilst that of the bird (gallinaceous) did not present these characters at all. As to man and other mammalia, six grains of finely-powdered, dry human blood, were put into a glass, and nine grains of phosphoric acid added. The blood, on being agitated with a glass rod, swelled and softened, turned into a brilliant mass of a hepatic colour, and as consistent as a common extract, but glutinous and devoid of plasticity. On being pressed with the rod, it yielded without dividing, and became more homogeneous; when allowed to stand it became hard without losing its lustre. The blood of the horse gave very different results. The acid first swelled and softened the powder, but the particles, far from forming themselves into a mass, turned into hard and shining lumps, which did not adhere to each other, and even broke asunder when attempts were made to unite them. The blood of the ox, calf, mule, pig, goat, &c., gave the same results as that of the horse. The blood of the cat formed a single mass like that of the man, but it broke at the slightest touch. Human blood always exhibits definite characters, notwithstanding differences of age, sex, health, or disease; except, however, as regards catamenial blood, which, although it gathers up into a mass, divides very soon into dry and swelled particles, that show no tendency to reunite.[1]

A simple means of distinguishing the blood of different animals was proposed by Gallicano Bertazzi,[2] who based his researches on the behaviour of iodine water on the contents (hæmatin and blood casein) of blood corpuscles.

---

[1] Lancet, 1849, vol. i. p. 348.

[2] Annali Univer. di Med. Aprile, 1839.

After preparing a saturated solution of iodine in water, he experimented in the following manner: A circular piece, five lines in diameter, is cut out of the spotted cloth and covered with 20 grains (1.25 gramme) of water; when the colouring matter is dissolved, the stuff is removed with the forceps, pressed out and treated with 10 grains of iodine water. A solution of bird's blood prepared in this manner, according to him, will change to reddish-brown, be troubled, and yield an abundant precipitate; a solution with that of carnivora turns reddish without showing any cloudiness or deposit, whilst with that of the herbivora, it only takes on a colour resembling cyprus wine. In order to produce the same effect with the blood of carnivora and human blood, 20, and with the herbivora 40 grains of iodine water must be added. With the blood of birds and carnivora the precipitate obtained is reddish-brown, and becomes red in the air, by degrees resembling cochineal; that of the last (herbivora) at first dark-red, becomes changed to chestnut-brown in the atmosphere.

By Specific Odour.—For the purpose of discriminating between different kinds of blood, on several occasions recourse has been made to the odour evolved by the addition of sulphuric acid. M. Barruel,[1] in 1829, when trying to obtain some of the colouring matter from ox blood, was struck with the peculiar animal odour developed on the addition of sulphuric acid to fresh blood, and subsequently in treating human blood in the same manner, the smell, resembling human sweat, was so powerful as to drive him from the laboratory. This discovery led him to make several experiments, with the following conclusions:—

[1] Annales d'Hygiène pub., t. i. p. 267.

1. That the blood of every animal contains a peculiar odorous principle; that of the male strong, of the female like it, but more feeble.

2. This principle is exceedingly volatile, and has a similar and peculiar smell of the sweat or vapour of the skin or lungs of the animal under consideration.

3. This principle is intimately combined with the blood, and not perceptible as long as the combination remains, but when this is destroyed the odorous principle of the blood evaporates and develops the characteristic smell of the animal from which it is derived.

4. This development is best obtained by means of sulphuric acid. The result is obtained by adding to one part of blood one and a half part (by measure) of concentrated sulphuric acid, and stirring the mixture with a glass rod. There is an elevation of temperature of the mass, during the process, when the peculiar smell is produced.

The researches elaborated by Barruel were in some degree confirmed by Taddei de Gravina,[1] who experimented with the blood of the ox, cow, and very young calf, an old and a very young hare, the goat, sheep, hog, horse and mare, man and woman, and numerous species of birds. From his various experiments he arrived at the following results: 1st. That it is true that the blood of every vertebrate animal has in it an odoriferous principle, identical in all individuals of the same species, and similar to the odour of the cutaneous transpirations, or more properly speaking, of that part of it which gives to each animal its characteristic smell. 2d. That the notion of those who pretend to recognize to which, among a number of individuals of the same species, a given portion of blood belongs, is false.

Carl Schmidt[1] made numerous experiments upon the odour of the blood of man, the dog, cat, calf, sheep, hog, goat, cat, besides those of hens and frogs, together with that of various animals of the different classes. To avoid the difficulties in this kind of investigation, the examination took place in the presence of six intelligent persons, who were requested to communicate their decision. During the trial they detected many kinds of blood with great accuracy and agreement, but throughout there was not much constancy in their opinions. In fine, that the method of Barruel is, under all circumstances, characteristic only with the blood of the goat, sheep, and cat, whilst with all the others very doubtful results are given.

A case occurred in which a man was charged with an assassination, at whose house was found a bucking cloth presenting many grayish stains. It was required to decide if these spots were owing to human blood, or, as the prisoner contended, they were produced by meat which he had enveloped in the cloth the year before to shield it from the flies. MM. Chevalier and Barruel were charged with the examination, and among other tests used that by odour. After making a solution of the stains, concentrating it at a low temperature, and mixing this with concentrated sulphuric acid, a slight odour resembling the smell of mutton was eliminated. While this opinion

[1] Die Diagnostik verdächtiger Flecke in Criminalfällen. Mitau und Leipzig, 1848, s. 19.

went far to admit the declaration of the accused, these gentlemen stated before the tribunal, the difficulty of deciding by this means, and the insufficiency of their evidence, requiring the court to rely upon other testimony for a verdict.[1]

Some few years ago MM. Tardieu, Barruel, and Chevalier, were required to decide if blood found in the house of a woman, who was accused of murder, was human, or, as she said, that of a sheep. The substance in question was submitted to the action of sulphuric acid in order to produce the peculiar odour. The disagreement between these experts was so great as to produce complete confusion in their own minds, and to destroy the confidence which had for a time been reposed in this test.[2]

It would be of the greatest value to be able by any means, however difficult or tedious, to distinguish the blood of one animal from that of another. Barruel[3] himself has admitted that his formula does not afford the certainty required in medico-legal investigation, and even for an approximation to a satisfactory result a large quantity of fresh blood is needed.

In the majority of assassinations a great length of time elapses between the commission of the deed and the examination of the suspected stains, and the quantity of blood presented is exceedingly small. To succeed by Barruel's method would require a more exquisitely cultivated sense of smell than is possessed by many persons. The difficulties and embarrassments by which this formula is surrounded, render it, for almost all ordinary cases,

[1] Annales d'Hygiène pub., t. x. 1833, p. 160.
[2] Ibid., t. xlix. 1853. p. 413.   [3] Ibid., t. xxiii. 1840. p. 396.

nearly useless, and in the few in which it can be employed, it holds a doubtful position. There have been many experiments performed according to the method of Barruel, with different kinds of blood, and the results of the observations by Couerbe, Leuret, Rudekind, Erhard, Merk, Soubeiran, Denis, and Chevalier, have shown, by the present means it is not possible in a medico-legal investigation, to distinguish human blood from that of animals by the odour evolved from that fluid.[1] Dr. Alfred S. Taylor takes occasion to say that after many trials with Barruel's process, he could come to no other conclusion than that it furnishes no criterion whatever, and that it would be dangerous to rely upon it in any case.[2]

Stains which may be confounded with Blood Stains.

The substances producing stains resembling, in a greater or less degree, those produced by blood, are exceedingly numerous, and it is very difficult to classify them satisfactorily. The appearance and reaction of stains made by metallic and vegetable dyes are often so modified by the presence of mordants or other chemicals, as to be difficult to recognize, and on this account each medico-legal examination, to a certain degree, must be studied by itself according to the circumstances which are presented.

Insoluble in Water.—From the chief characteristic of blood stains—solubility in water—the substances of this class are readily distinguished. The principal of these are dragon's blood. Venetian red (Indian red), red ochre

---

[1] Journal de Chimie Méd., tom. v. 2me ser., p. 493.

[2] Remarks on the Trial of Thomas Drury. Guy's Hospital Reports, vol. vii. p. 372.

(Spanish brown), vermilion, alkanet, precipitated carbonate of iron, colcothar, and iron rust.

Soluble in Water.—Madder. This substance, used very much in dyeing, imparts to water a brownish colour, which is made crimson by addition of ammonia, and yellow by sulphuric and muriatic acids. This dye has obtained more notice since M. Raspail,[1] in a memoir read before the Académie Royale, contested the value of the chemical characters of blood, and, according to him, these properties very well suffice to prove that a stain of blood is not a stain of rust, citrate of iron, cochineal, madder, &c., but they are not sufficient to show that the stain is truly of blood. He gave as proof, that having spotted linen and glass with white of egg which had remained for several hours in a linen bag with madder in powder, which had been previously moistened, the stains behaved towards reagents in the same manner as it had been said blood stains reacted. These assertions of Raspail were completely refuted by M. Orfila,[2] who showed the difference of reaction by several means, and among them:—

1. That solution of alum and proto-chloride of tin only dilute the colour of blood, while the mixture of albumen and madder is rendered yellow by their solutions.

2. That the colour of a mixture of albumen and madder is not destroyed by heat, when boiled together, as is seen constantly in dye-houses, where madder would be nearly useless if its brilliancy were so easily injured.

In comparative experiments with a mixture of albumen with madder and colour of the blood, it is necessary to be

[1] Archives Gén., 1828, t. xvi. p. 299.
[2] Ibid., p. 161.

careful that the latter contains no agent which prevents the loss of colour by heat, for, by neglect of this, the discrimination may be doubtful.

Sanguinaria readily yields its colour to water, and the solution bears a great similarity to blood. Its solution is coagulated and rendered bright crimson by addition of sulphuric and nitric acids, and completely decolourized by the addition of ammonia and potassa.

Brazil Wood.—The colour of an aqueous solution of Brazil wood is a dark-brown, and is made crimson by ammonia, sulphuric and muriatic acids, and is deepened by bichromate of potassa. Logwood, the dye most frequent in domestic use, readily yields its colour to water, and the solution, which is a dark-brown inclining to purple, is deepened by ammonia, reddened by sulphuric acid, instantly changed black by solution of sulphate of iron, and blue by acetate of copper.

Camwood and Red Saunders are but slightly soluble in cold, more soluble in hot water, and rapidly so in acetic acid, alcohol, ether, and alkaline solutions. The colour is rendered violet-red by ammonia and potassa, and rose-red by sulphuric acid.

Archil (Cudbear).—Fruit stains, and the stains of plants and flowers, are changed to blue and green by ammonia.

Sulpho-Cyanate of Iron, mixed with albumen, gives to water a striking resemblance to a solution of blood, but is instantly decolourized by addition of ammonia.

Stains soluble in Water and unchanged by Ammonia.

Citrate of Iron.—When blood in a thin stratum is dried upon a porcelain plate, it shrinks and forms scales which are not unlike this preparation. The colour of the solution of citrate of iron is deepened in the same manner as blood, but is quickly destroyed by addition of sulphuric acid, which decomposes the salt.

Anatto, dissolved in water, imparts an orange-yellow colour to water which is not decolourized by heat. The stain produced by this colouring matter is instantly changed to a dark-blue by addition of sulphuric and nitric acids.

Catechu, Rhatany, and Kino.—These substances form with water dark-brown solutions, and owing to the presence of tannin in large proportion, they can be with ease distinguished from blood. By the addition of a salt of iron, the latter becomes green, while, with the first two, the solution is changed to black.

By a careful and minute comparison of the action of the various colours simulating blood, when treated by the different reagents, with the characteristics of blood under the same circumstances, it is seen that as yet no substance has been found which cannot be distinguished from it without difficulty, where sufficient care and accuracy have been regarded in the experiments.

II. MICROSCOPICAL EXAMINATION OF BLOOD STAINS.

For some years past, the microscope has been resorted to, in order to distinguish fluids resembling blood, reddish stains of a suspicious character, and the blood of one animal from that of another. In no kind of investigation has the use of the microscope met with less opposition, and its merits so rarely called in question, as in medico-legal evidence. Without this instrument many criminals would have escaped punishment, for, by its use, evidence,

7

which was surrounded by doubts and difficulties, has been made substantial and clear, and frequently, things that were supposed of no moment, by its employment have been found connecting corroborative circumstances, which, till then, seemed to have no relation whatever. The rapidity and accuracy with which blood can be recognized in a microscope of good construction, commend themselves in a question requiring all possible certainty for its solution. The microscope not only furnishes the means of examining and defining objects invisible to the eye, but enables us to make, with facility, microscopico-chemical researches of the highest importance to the chemist and physiologist.

It is needless to add, that familiarity with the instrument, and the substances to be examined, is requisite to derive the advantages which it possesses.

BLOOD.—The blood is a slightly tenacious fluid of a specific gravity of 1.055, and, when drawn from the vessels, presents to the eye a bright cherry-red colour, uniform in aspect, and separating, after a time, into crassamentum and serum. When examined in the microscope, its peculiar bodies, the corpuscles, are seen floating in the *liquor sanguinis*, giving it the appearance of an emulsion, which, when the blood is traversing the vessels, permits us to note the course and its rate of movement. In the blood, three different forms of bodies have been discovered constantly present—the red globules or corpuscles, the white, and a smaller kind called molecules. For these, many different names have been given by distinguished observers, but here I shall retain those in common use.

Red Corpuscles.—The red corpuscles, which bear the colouring matter of the blood, are, in man, shining, circular, slightly bi-concave cells, without a nucleus, and so numerous that to observe them satisfactorily, the blood requires to be diluted in some degree, or spread in an extremely thin layer. The colour of a single corpuscle, when viewed by transmitted light, is a dusky-yellow, but when piled one above another in mass, they are red. When the corpuscle lies on its edge, a bright-yellowish line only is seen. The diameter of a human corpuscle averages, according to the measurement of Hassall,[1] about $\frac{1}{3500}$ of an inch, and sometimes they can be found much larger. The number of corpuscles which exceed in size or fall below the standard, has been estimated by Carl Schmidt, to be only two per cent., so that the deviation scarcely affects the appearance presented to the eye in the field of the microscope. During the coagulation of the blood, the globules form into piles resembling coins, and by desiccation of the walls shrink upon their contents, giving them a stellar form; the same result occurs when blood is mixed with urine and allowed to remain for some hours. The membrane of the corpuscle is very elastic, exceedingly delicate in structure, and is quickly affected by the action of reagents. In common with animal membranes, the corpuscles possess, in a high degree, the physical property discovered by Dutrochet, of endosmosis and exosmosis, which renders them susceptible of rapid change in size and shape, and consequently in diameter, on the addition of a fluid having a different specific

[1] Microscopic Anatomy (Am. ed.), vol. i. p. 91.

gravity from that of the blood, that demands an attentive consideration from the medico-legal examiner.

On the addition of a small quantity of water, the corpuscles become thicker, and when more water is added they swell, assume a spherical form and burst, discharging their contents, leaving behind a circular line, as it were, its border. The same result follows when alcohol, ether, and creasote are added, but, at the same time, the corpuscles are rendered so transparent as with difficulty to be found. Potassa, soda, and ammonia in dilute solutions dissolve them. Phosphate, carbonate and sulphate of soda preserve their shape and slightly increase their size. Acetic acid extracts the colouring matter from the corpuscles, renders them white and perfectly transparent, and by degrees dissolves the membrane completely. By the tincture of iodine they are not altered in form, but the outline becomes more distinct. In a strong solution of corrosive sublimate, the corpuscles undergo no change of shape, but they have a more sharply defined outline, and can be preserved in this for a long time. Chloroform makes the globules bright yellow, causes the centre to appear and the outline to be indistinct.

The blood-corpuscles are distinguished by peculiarities of form and size in the different classes of animals, that may enable us to recognize to what animal a certain specimen of blood belongs. In this respect, the microscope alone can aid us, since chemistry furnishes no means of estimating the shape and diameter of the corpuscles. In the mammalia, the corpuscles are circular, and without nuclei, except in the elephant, camel, dromedary, and lama, where they are found elliptical, bi-convex, and containing nuclei. In birds, the corpuscles are elongated and fusiform in shape, with well-defined outline and nucleus; and in the amphibia, they are oval, plainly convex, and have perceptible nuclei. The blood-corpuscles of embryonic life[1] are larger, and sometimes as large again, as in the animal after respiration has been established, and present themselves in the shape of soft, round, but often irregular bodies, of a pale red colour.

In order to obtain precise knowledge of the exact size of the corpuscles in different animals, resort has been made to micrometry by many celebrated observers, and the measurement of a number of specimens of each variety noted, to furnish data for accurate comparison. Latterly, for legal purposes, Carl Schmidt[2] has, with great assiduity and astonishing perseverance, accomplished the task, and below will be found the result of his experiments with forty different specimens of blood of the animals named, except with that of the rat, mouse, frog, and chicken, in which there were twenty.

The plan he at first adopted, was by drying blood in very thin layers upon glass plates. The size is given in millimetres, and the measurements of Gulliver are appended.

[1] R. Wagner's Physiology by Willis, Lond. 1841, p. 248.
[2] Op. cit., nebenstehende Tafel.

1. *Blood-globules Dried in thin layers, on Glass Slides.*

	Man.	Dog.	Rabbit	Rat.	Pig.	Mouse.	Ox.	Cat.	Horse.	Sheep.
Mean	0.0077	0.0070	0.0064	0.0064	0.0062	0.0061	0.0058	0.0056	0.0057	0.0045
Minimum . .	0.0074	0.0066	0.0060	0.0060	0.0060	0.0058	0.0054	0.0053	0.0053	0.0040
Maximum . .	0.0080	0.0074	0.0070	0.0068	0.0065	0.0065	0.0062	0.0060	0.0060	0.0048
AFTER GULLIVER.										
Mean	0.0074	0.0072	0.0070	0.0068	0.0060	0.0067	0.0060	0.0058	0.0054	0.0055
Minimum. . . .	..	0.0056	0.0051	0.0048	0.0048	0.0048	0.0048	0.0054	0.0048	0.0032
Maximum . .	..	0.0088	0.0095	0.0085	0.0071	0.0085	0.0071	0.0064	0.0072	0.0064

			Mean.	Minimum:	Maximum.
Chicken	Broadth	. . . . . .	0.0076	0.0070	0.0081
	Length	. . . . . .	0.0127	0.0120	0.0135
Frog .	Breadth	. . . . . .	0.0154	0.0142	0.0157
	Length	. . . . . .	0.0211	0.0201	0.0220

To more closely approach standard measures for criminal cases, he experimented with blood dried in mass, and
obtained the following:—

2. *Blood-globules Dried in Mass, on Wood and other Substances.*

	Man.	Pig.	Ox.	Horse.	Sheep.	Chicken.	
						Breadth.	Length.
Mean	0.0040	0.0034	0.0030	0.0028	0.0022	0.0040	0.0074
Minimum	0.0037	0.0030	0.0028	0.0026	0.0020	0.0038	0.0070
Maximum	0.0045	0.0037	0.0031	0.0031	0.0025	0.0042	0.0078

White Corpuscles.—With the red globules are found
colourless corpuscles, which are far less numerous, but
subject to great increase and diminution in their relative
proportion to one another under various circumstances,
and more numerous than would be supposed from the
careless observation of a single specimen of healthy blood.

The white corpuscles are very delicate and highly elastic cells, globular in form in all kinds of blood, when not subjected to pressure, with a clear, shining border, and slightly granular appearance in structure, containing nuclei varying in number. The term white, only serves as a distinction of the different bodies in red-blooded animals, for in insects the globules are all colourless, yet they are of different sizes. The white corpuscles have an average diameter of $\frac{1}{2570}$ of an inch; in the mammalia they are larger than the red, while in frogs they are smaller.

When submitted to the action of acetic acid, the outline is rendered transparent, the internal structure is coagulated, and the nuclei—which, having a slightly reddish-yellow tinge, become visible—seem to unite and adhere together. By the addition of water, they enlarge in size without alteration in form, when the granules plainly appear, resembling pus-globules in a striking manner. When to blood under examination, water is cautiously added, the red corpuscles soon swell and burst, while the colourless ones are made perceptible, though before hid from the eye by the mass covering them.

The number of white corpuscles is small compared with the red, and, according to the careful enumerations made by Moleschott[1] with the blood of different individuals, was 1: 314; so that a specimen of healthy blood shows but a few of them in the field of the microscope. This proportion is, however, liable to great alteration; and in the disease first noted by Virchow, and denominated leukæmia, and independently, and almost simultaneously discovered by J. H. Bennett, and by him called leuco-

[1] Lehmann's Physiol. Chemistry, Am. ed., vol. i, p. 611.

cythemia, the ratio is increased in some cases as high as 1 : 3.

Some years ago, when studying this disease, or, more properly speaking, condition of the blood, I was surprised at the destruction and total disappearance of the colourless corpuscles, when the process of desiccation had taken place, and that it was impossible to reproduce them in their normal state. My opinion in this respect, I find confirmed by the eminent microscopist, Ch. Robin,[1] who says that, "in blood which begins to dry, the white corpuscles change their shape; their surface, which is more dense than the central portion, breaks and allows the contents to escape." It has been asserted by Prof. Wyman,[2] "that by examination of blood dried on glass, painted wood, &c., to which water is added, after a careful inspection, the observer will seldom be able to find any traces of blood-disks; but transparent, colourless spots will be seen scattered through the mass, which, with a high power (say 800 diameters), may be seen to have a globular form and to contain granules—usually three or four. These are the lymph corpuscles."

It is difficult to reconcile the remarks of Prof. Wyman with the rupture of the white corpuscles by drying, and I have tried again and again the experiment as described by him, and have not yet been able to discover in the dried blood any lymph corpuscles with their nuclei. Presumptuous as it may appear to doubt the accuracy of his observation, yet as the opinion, which I believe to be

[1] Briand, Med. Legale, p. 788.

[2] Note by Prof. Wyman in the Report of the Case of Jno. W. Webster. Boston, 1850, p. 90.

erroneous, has already found place, unchallenged, in a work[1] of high standing, it is admissible to call it in question. The red corpuscles of the blood, when treated with water, become decolourized, as has been shown by L. Mandl,[2] in one of the first contributions on the subject, who says: "It is known that the globules of the blood, placed in water, are deprived of colour, and leave only a white bed formed of fibrin. The blood-globules having lost their colour entirely, there remains no indication whether or not they are from the blood of a mammifera, since, in the fluid drawn from an ovipara, oblong nuclei, in great number, are seen in the midst of the white layer of fibrin." The same result takes place, I think, when dried blood is inspected in the same way, which explains the discrepancy of opinion held on the subject.

Molecules.—These minute spherical bodies of the blood do not enter into forensic investigations, and, consequently, require no consideration here.

Derivation of Blood.—It frequently happens, in murder trials, when blood has been too plainly visible on the clothing of the prisoner, there is a defence made, explaining its presence by the killing of some animal, or by some natural cause. This can sometimes be contradicted, by finding mixed with the blood some substance which serves to denote its origin, as shown in a trial at Norwich, England, a few years ago.[3] A female child, nine years old, was found lying on the ground, in a small plantation,

---

[1] Wharton and Stillé Med. Jurisprudence, p. 562.

[2] Recher. Méd. légales sur le Sang, Thèse de Paris, 1842.

[3] Chambers's Journal, part xxxv. Dec. 1856.

quite dead, with a large and deep gash in the throat. Suspicion fell upon the mother of the murdered girl, who, upon being taken into custody, behaved with the utmost coolness, and admitted having taken her child to the plantation where the body was found, whence the child was lost by getting separated while in quest of flowers. Upon being searched, there was found in the woman's possession a large and sharp knife, which was at once subjected to minute and careful examination. Nothing, however, was found upon it, with the exception of a few pieces of hair adhering to the handle, so exceedingly small as scarcely to be visible. The examination being conducted in the presence of the prisoner, and the officer remarking: "Here is a bit of fur or hair on the handle of your knife," the woman immediately replied: "Yes, I dare say there is, and very likely some stains of blood, for, as I came home, I found a rabbit caught in a snare, and cut its throat with the knife." The knife was sent to London, and, with the particles of hair, subjected to a microscopic examination. No trace of blood could at first be detected upon the weapon, which appeared to have been washed; but, upon separating the horn handle from its iron lining, it was found that, between the two, a fluid had penetrated, which turned out to be blood—certainly not the blood of a rabbit, but bearing every resemblance to that of the human body. The hair was then submitted to examination. Without knowing anything of the facts of the case, the microscopist immediately declared the hair to be that of a *squirrel*. Now, round the neck of the child, at the time of the murder, there was a tippet or "victorine," over which the knife, by whomever held, must have glided; and this victorine was of *squirrel's fur!*

This strong circumstantial evidence of the guilt of the prisoner, was deemed by the jury sufficient for a conviction, and, whilst awaiting execution, the wretched woman fully confessed her crime.

When blood is said to be derived from hemorrhages of various kinds, the truth or falsity of the statement can sometimes be found, by the discovery of a structure mixed therewith, peculiar to a certain part of the body, indicating its exact source. When from the nostril or lungs, by the admixture of the ciliary, and from the stomach and intestines, the columnar, epithelium. When from the bowels, by the presence of bile and feculent matter; and from the urinary bladder, by the salts contained in urine. Menstrual blood is detected by the pavement epithelium peculiar to the vagina.

Where fracture of the skull has been produced, the mixture of blood and brain matter known by the characteristic nerve-cells, found upon a bludgeon or other weapon, marks it as the destructive instrument. Should the polygonal cells of the liver be upon a knife supposed to have been used where a man has been stabbed in that organ, it would confirm suspicion.

If the charge of stupration be brought, and blood stains containing spermatozoa produced, it would be strong evidence that the crime had been committed, though, at the same time, it is not difficult to imagine that sperm could be obtained and surreptitiously mixed with blood in order to sustain a false accusation.

In like manner many other things and circumstances could be named where the presence of other substances with blood would elucidate the investigation of a case; but as they are so numerous, I have contented myself by enumerating a few of them.

BLOOD-CRYSTALS.—The colouring matter which in the blood remains in solution, when under favorable circumstances, is changed, and becomes a crystallizable material, furnishing crystals of beautiful colour and form. The merit of their discovery is granted to O. Funke, who was very soon followed by F. Kunde, who succeeded in obtaining crystals from many different kinds of blood. It is most wonderful that this peculiar substance does not yield the same form of crystal in blood belonging to all classes of animals, which places within our reach a novel mode of recognizing in some cases, by the shape of crystallization obtained, to what animal a certain specimen of blood belongs, a fact not to be disregarded by the careful analyst who brings all knowledge to bear on the question.

This interesting subject has received much attention from Lehmann,[1] who says the crystals occur in three forms—namely, in prisms, tetrahedra, and hexagonal tablets. The prismatic forms, whose true system of crystallization has not been firmly established, notwithstanding the attention which has been devoted to the subject, are peculiar to human blood and to the blood of most mammals and fishes; the tetrahedra are met with in some of the rodents—as, for instance, in guinea-pigs, rats, and mice; while the hexagonal tablets have hitherto been found only in squirrels. A glance at this attractive sub-

[1] Op. cit., vol. i. p. 344.

ject at once shows the advantage which could be gained by resort to the crystallization of blood to determine its derivation.

The method of obtaining crystals is to put a drop of blood on a glass slide, add a small quantity of water, alcohol, or ether, and then allow evaporation to take place slightly, covering it with a glass slip, first interposing a hair between the glasses, to afford room for the crystallization, when carmine-red crystals of different sizes will appear in from half an hour to a few hours or several days, according to the kind of blood and the situation in which it has been placed. The crystals are more rapidly obtained by exposure to sunlight, and more easily from defibrinated blood. The shortest time in which I have noted their formation was in half an hour, from the blood of a rat. The glass slip is not necessary, but very convenient in producing them, especially for the first essay, since they form quite well when exposed to the air and sunlight; a little difficulty lies in knowing the proper quantity of water or other fluid to be added.

Besides the bright-red crystals peculiar to blood, are seen consociated those of chloride of sodium and phosphate of soda, which are found when either fresh or dried blood is submitted to the process of crystallization.

The blood from which it is desired to make crystals does not require to be taken immediately from the vessels, but they are with less trouble procured when it has stood from twelve to twenty-four hours; which is a great advantage when demanded in legal cases. It is somewhat difficult to preserve the crystals for a length of time perfect in form, and the best plan is by Canada balsam. I have, however, been able to keep them for several months, well enough to recognize them, by having so much blood and water on the plate, that, when the glass cover is applied, the fluid will form a rim around the specimen, by the drying of which the object is sealed from atmospheric influence. It would appear that crystals are sometimes preserved in a like manner when they form in clots, and there is no more certain mode of identifying blood than by finding them.

In an instance where blood stains on cloth had remained for twenty-one months exposed to the atmosphere, Friedberg[1] found this special kind of crystals, which he calls hæmatin-crystals; and so very characteristic, that, in his opinion, one can with most perfect assurance prove the presence of blood when they are seen. Care must be taken not to mistake for them minute lamina, found in clots upon hard substances, whose accidental shape, when seen by a low power, sometimes simulates crystals.

From blood which has been kept in dried clots for several months I have tried many times to obtain crystals, and lately have been successful in making some from ox blood, preserved as above stated; which, however, were not very perfect specimens of crystallization. At the same time this is somewhat mortifying to acknowledge, yet it gives encouragement and desire for further experiment. The plan adopted was to dissolve the clot in water, and allow it to stand until the corpuscles had all burst, then filtering the solution, and, after the addition of ether or chloroform, proceed as with fresh blood.

DRIED BLOOD.—The vital fluid is so constituted as to

[1] Histologie des Blutes, Berlin, 1852, s. 71.

possess an inherent power of self-preservation, whereby the anatomical constituent, the red corpuscles, provided no putrefaction has taken place, is retained by desiccation in such a state that, upon the addition of certain fluids, the normal condition of the globules can be almost perfectly restored. Blood has been kept by many observers for different periods of time, and some as long as nine years, with no perceptible alteration. Before me are several specimens put away for five years, not having changed at all, without any further care than to keep them dry.

The time required to soften the blood to such a degree as to reproduce the corpuscles, varies from a few minutes to several hours, and is proportioned to the age of the clot and the tenuity or solubility of the reagent employed. Owing to the rapid endosmotic action which is found to take place in the corpuscles when a fluid whose density is lower than that of the serum is added to blood, by which they swell and soon burst, destroying their identity, some trouble has been experienced in the selection of menstrua which would most suitably answer the two purposes—of moistening the mass, and reinstating the corpuscles. For this purpose a great variety of fluids have been suggested and used, some of which have been esteemed by one observer, and disliked by another.

Water.—In dried blood, where no decomposition has taken place, it has parted with its water by evaporation; and it will readily occur to any one that by the cautious addition of water, in quantity proportioned to the size of the stain, a close imitation of the normal serum is made. When water is used, many of the corpuscles are sacrificed before its density has been raised, by the salts and other elements of the blood, to that of serum; and when this has been done, the globules are seen floating about, with well-defined outline. This reagent is more particularly useful when the stain is very old, for in recent specimens, when submitted to its action, the endosmosis is so violent as to destroy the corpuscles. There is perhaps no fluid in use for softening masses of blood which requires more care and experience than water, and it is well to take the precaution to scrape a small portion of a clot on to a slide, and, after placing the same in the field of the instrument, add the water, when the reaction can be observed.

Serum.—The objection to the use of serum is the difficulty of obtaining it entirely free from corpuscles; and to obviate this, the contents of hydroceles have been employed. That serum might be applied to this purpose, F. W. Böcker[1] has, very ingeniously, proposed to filter human or other mammalian blood, and to use the serum thus obtained for the examination of frog's blood, or that of the ovipara; and in like manner, to take the serum of frog's blood to mix with the blood having round corpuscles.

Albumen.—This substance, as presented in the white of an egg, has been taken for the microscopic examination of blood, and has been found free from many objections belonging to other substances.

Glycerine. — This menstruum has been highly commended by Dr. Alf. S. Taylor,[2] on account of its close

[1] Memoranda der gerichtlichen Medizin, Iserlohn, 1854, s. 281.
[2] Medical Jurisprudence, 4th Am. ed., p. 239.

approach in specific gravity to that of serum, and the slowness with which it evaporates. The ease of obtaining glycerine of purity is another advantage which it possesses. With albumen and glycerine a slight refraction of light takes place, which might disturb the vision of one unaccustomed to microscopy.

Besides the above, oil, solutions of sugar and sulphate of soda, liquor amnii, and an aqueous solution of iodine, to which sugar has been added, have been used by different individuals for bringing the corpuscles in relief, and allowing them to be quickly recognized, but none are so free from objection as albumen and glycerine.

The blood corpuscles can be preserved so well for several years, that they retain their characteristic shape, and indicate accurately the race of animal to which they belong, by simply spreading them on a glass slide, in a very thin layer, when, by blowing upon them, or waving the slide back and forth in the air, to make vaporization take place rapidly, these bodies are fixed, and may be permanently prepared by putting a frame of gold size around them, and applying a cover. The contraction of the contents takes place equally on all sides, whereby their form is preserved.

Carl Schmidt[1] is of opinion that "the drying of blood globules of different animals, isolated or in mass, adheres to the same rule of evaporation as the pollen of a flower, and the coefficient of desiccation in all of them bears a constant relation to the diminution of their volume. The micrometric definition proves this presumption, and gives us the solution of the most difficult problem on this point,

[1] Op. cit., s. 5.

the diagnosis of certain kinds of animal blood, in a dried condition, from one another and from that of man." This plausible and philosophical opinion seems to forestall any doubts or difficulties which might be raised from inspecting dried blood, and unfortunately it is not fully borne out in all practical cases, forcing one, however enthusiastic he may be to claim for the microscope the highest merited confidence, to acknowledge there are circumstances when it fails to discriminate positively the dried blood of one animal from that of another.

Some alteration in the form of the corpuscles is produced by drying upon substances of a porous nature, whereby their integrity is injured. In the Marylebone Police Court, in the case of Wm. Styles, Dr. Hassall[1] made the following remarks directly bearing on this question : While the determination, by means of the microscope, of the nature of blood stains, even when very recent, formed on cloth, linen, and other soft and porous textures, is usually a matter of considerable difficulty, and is often impossible, the determination of such stains, however old, as are placed on glass, porcelain, wood, and other hard or smooth surfaces, is in general unattended with difficulty, and extremely satisfactory. This difference is to be explained thus: in the one case the fibrin, albumen, and serum of the blood are in part absorbed and pass into the cavities of the hairs or fibres of the wool or linen; the blood corpuscles are thus deprived of their preservative fluids and shrink up—become misshapen or disintegrated; while in the other case the fibrin and al-

[1] Lancet for 1852, vol. i. p. 321.

bumen harden around the blood-disks in drying, and thus preserve them slightly altered in form only.

The difficulty is further well illustrated in the following case: A man walking alone on the street, received a blow in the face which stunned him and caused the blood to flow; on recovering, he found himself robbed of his money. A labourer was arrested on suspicion, on whose pantaloons was found a large blood stain, which, he said, was produced in helping to kill a cow. The stained garment was submitted to microscopical examination, in which Profs. Du Bois and Reymond participated. Answer of committee: Blood corpuscles of ox blood can only be discriminated from human blood corpuscles by their smaller size. On examining fresh blood of oxen and fresh blood of man, the human corpuscles are found to be larger, and could be easily recognized even on admixture with the smaller ones of ox blood. Some threads saturated with blood were cautiously taken out of the blood stained pantaloons and macerated in pure bone oil: on bringing the preparation under the microscope, the form of the blood corpuscles was found too indistinct to warrant a conclusion as to their nature. The blood stain was at least three, if not six, weeks old, at which time the corpuscles have acquired their shrivelled appearance, which always gives uncertain results. In order to examine the opposite opinion of Schmidt, the following experiment was made: fresh human and fresh ox blood was put upon the pantaloons, and allowed to dry for a week. The blood stains were then softened in bone oil, and brought separately and mixed up under the microscope. It seemed as if the dried human blood had more resemblance to the blood found on the garment than the dried blood of the ox, but the form and diameter of both kinds of blood-corpuscles were so much changed by shrivelling, that conscientiously a discrimination could not be made.[1]

Böcker[2] says that "sometimes by the drying of blood the corpuscles are destroyed, when only shapeless little masses or roundish granules remain, whose true nature it is impossible to discover microscopically. I have among others, a specimem of dried pigeon blood, three years old, in which I and several practiced microscopists cannot discover a single elliptical or oval blood globule, whilst very many round granules of the size of human corpuscles are seen. Moreover, I have found the bird's dried blood, when moistened with a solution of sugar, or in fresh filtered serum of frog's blood, contains a great many round, indeed, chiefly round, corpuscles very similar to those of human blood, and it is often necessary to search a long while before an elliptical one is found. In human and mammalian dried blood, I have never found elliptical blood corpuscles."

After numerous and carefully conducted experiments, Friedberg[3] mournfully acknowledges "that the solution of the most difficult problem—the diagnosis of the blood of man and certain mammalia, in a dried state, as Schmidt has announced as positive in all cases—is still a *pium desiderium*, and it is not possible by the present known means of examination to distinguish them, as the results of the many systematic experiments I have made authorize me in saying."

[1] Op. cit., von J. L. Casper, s. 157.
[2] Op. cit., s. 282.   [3] Op. cit., s. 57.

Ritter,[1] in his well digested and carefully arranged prize essay, takes occasion to remark that, "in his researches he has not found the facts as interpreted by Schmidt, and agrees with the conclusions of Friedberg."

From the experiments which I have made during a period of several years with blood belonging to different animals, when dried for a length of time and moistened again, I am forced to admit that great difficulty arises in attempting to fix its origin by the comparative size of the corpuscles; and again, that the blood of ovipara, when kept for several weeks, does not present the peculiar elliptical corpuscles, found in fresh blood, in a form sufficiently perfect to justify me in declaring positively whence it proceeds.

[1] Ueber die Ermittelung von Blut, Saamen, und Exrementenflecken in Kriminalfællen. Würzburg, 1854, s. 139.